Fuzzy Memories

Fuzzy Memories

by Jack Handey

ANDREWS AND MCMEEL
A Universal Press Syndicate Company
Kansas City

Library of Congress Cataloging-in-Publication Data
Handey, Jack, 1949–
    Fuzzy memories / by Jack Handey.
       p.   cm.
    ISBN 0-8362-1040-9 (alk. paper)
    1. American wit and humor.   I. Title
PN6162.H275   1996
818'.5402—dc20   95–49310
                                                            CIP

*Thanks to FPG International and SuperStock for use of the photos found in
this book. See page 120 for a full list of photo credits.*

Attention: Schools and Businesses
Andrews and McMeel books are available at quantity discounts with bulk
purchase for educational, business, or sales promotional use. For informa-
tion, please write to Special Sales Department, Andrews and McMeel, 4900
Main Street, Kansas City, Missouri 64112.

To my brother Terry

(1953–1995)

Special Thanks to:

Kit Boss
Joe and Mary Chavez
Mike Chavez
Becky Sue Epstein
John Fortenberry
Tom Gammill and Sandy Gillis
George Meyer and Maria Semple
Lorne Michaels
William, Linda, Ben, and Jesse Novak
Max Pross and Mira Velimirović

Thanks also to: my agent, Jim Trupin; my editor,
Jean Lowe; Thomas Thornton; Vickie Warr; and
most especially my wife and soul mate, Marta
Chavez Handey

I think the best Thanksgiving I ever had was the one where we didn't even have a turkey. Mom and Dad sat us kids down and explained that business hadn't been good at Dad's store, so we couldn't afford a turkey. We had vegetables and bread and pie, and it was just fine.

Later I went into Mom and Dad's bedroom to thank them, and I caught them eating a little turkey.

I guess that wasn't really the *best* Thanksgiving.

When we would go for a drive in the family car, I used to love to stick my head out the window, until one time we passed an oncoming car and my head knocked off a dog's head.

There used to be a house on our block that we thought was haunted, because you'd hear people screaming inside and because people who went in never came out. Later on we found out it was just a murderer's house.

"I'll take that little one, way in the back," I said.

"That little collie mix?" said the animal shelter guy.

"No," I said, "the one behind him."

"The gray terrier?" he said.

"He's gray," I said, "but way in the back, in the corner."

"You mean the water faucet?" he said. I realized then it *was* a water faucet, but I didn't want to look like a jerk, so I said, "Yeah, that's the one I want."

It ended up costing me almost five hundred dollars to get that faucet removed. But you know, I've still got that faucet, and I wouldn't trade it for any dog in the world.

When you're ten years old, and a car drives by and splashes a puddle of water all over you, it's hard to decide if you should go to school like that or try to go home and change and probably be late. So while he was trying to decide, I drove by and splashed him again.

For a while there, instead of calling Grandpa "Grandpa," I started calling him "Grandpappy." But he didn't like that, and asked me to go back to Grandpa. So I did, but I changed it a little. I put an "e" in instead of an "a," so it became "Grendpa."

At first he didn't notice, but then he said, "What did you call me?"

"Grandpa," I said. But then I went back to calling him Grendpa. Finally he just said to go ahead and call him Grandpappy, which I did, only I changed it a little bit to "Grendpeppy."

When I was seven, I told my friend Timmy Barker I would give him a million dollars if he would eat an earthworm. He ate the worm, but I never gave him the million dollars. As of last week, all I had given him was $9,840.

I didn't want to cut down that tree. But I had no choice. It was growing right where I'm going to build my house, if I can ever get enough money together to build it and if I also have enough money to buy the land. That's another thing: I need to find out who owns that land.

Mom used to make the most beautiful Easter eggs. Then she'd hide them in the backyard. But they were so beautiful, when we found one, we weren't allowed to pick it up. We had to point at it, and then Mom would come pick it up with her white gloves and put it back in its case.

Somebody ended up smashing all those eggs with a hammer. I think it was our dog.

I don't think I can be hypnotized. This hypnotist tried to hypnotize me one time, but he couldn't. And I tell him that each time I go over to wash his car, which is every Wednesday.

Sometimes kids are so cruel to animals, especially insects. I remember one time I caught this grasshopper, and I made him wear a little straw hat that I had made. Also a little pair of denim overalls. And I made him hold this little tiny pitchfork. So guess what he looked like? What is the enemy of the grasshopper and the one thing he wouldn't want to look like? That's right, a farmer.

As I felt the soft cool mud squish between my toes, I thought, Man, these are not very good shoes!

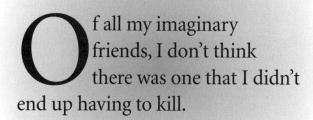

Of all my imaginary friends, I don't think there was one that I didn't end up having to kill.

Grandpa used to describe the size of every-thing in terms of a calf. For instance, if he was describing a large dog, he would say it was "about as big as a calf." Or about a car, he would say it "could seat four calves comfortably." (Oh, that was another thing: how many calves could ride in something.)

One time he was talking about a calf he had, and I asked him how big it was. He said it was "about three-quarters as big as a calf."

Sometimes Grandpa would tell time by calves. If you asked him how long something would take, he'd say, "About as long as it takes a calf to drive over here."

I remember I was hammering on a fence in the backyard when Dad approached. He was carrying a letter or something in his hand, and he looked worried.

I continued to hammer as he came toward me. "Son," he said, "why are you hammering on that fence? It already has plenty of nails in it."

"Oh, I'm not using nails," I replied. "I'm just hammering." With that, I returned to my hammering.

Dad asked me to stop hammering, as he had some news. I did stop hammering, but first I got a couple more hammers in, and this seemed to make Dad mad. "I said, stop hammering!" he yelled.

I think he felt bad for yelling at me, especially since it

looked like he had bad news. "Look," he said, "you can hammer later, but first—"

Well, I didn't even wait to hear the rest. As soon as I heard "You can hammer," that's what I started doing. Hammering away, happy as an old hammer dog.

Dad tried to physically stop me from hammering by inserting a small log of some sort between my hammer and the fence. But I just kept on hammering, 'cause that's the way I am when I get that hammer going. Then, he just grabbed my arm and made me stop.

"I'm afraid I have some news for you," he said.

I swear, what I did next was not hammering. I was just letting the hammer swing lazily at arm's length, and maybe it tapped the fence once or twice, but that's all. That apparently didn't make any difference whatsoever to Dad, because he just grabbed my hammer out of my hand and flung it across the field.

And when I saw my hammer flying helplessly through

the air like that, I just couldn't take it. I burst out crying, I admit it. And I ran to the house, as fast as my legs could take me.

"Son, come back!" yelled Dad. "What about your hammer?!"

But I could not have cared less about hammering at that point. I ran into the house and flung myself onto my bed, pounding the bed with my fists. I pounded and pounded, until finally, behind me, I heard a voice. "As long as you're pounding, why not use this?" I turned, and it was Dad, holding a brand-new solid-gold hammer.

I quickly wiped the tears from my eyes and ran to Dad's outstretched arms. But suddenly, he jumped out of the way, and I went sailing through the second-story window behind him.

Whenever I hear about a kid getting in trouble with drugs, I like to tell him this story.

Once, when I got lost in the woods, I was afraid that eventually I might have to eat Tippy. But finally I found my way home, and I was able to put Tippy back in the refrigerator with my other sandwiches.

Mom always told me I could be whatever I wanted to be when I grew up, "within reason." When I asked her what she meant by "within reason," she said, "You ask a lot of questions for a garbage man."

At first I thought a good way to get people to dig you some flower beds for free would be to call the police and say you buried some bodies in your backyard. But here's the catch: They dig *everywhere*, not just where you tell them to.

The day I met Marta was the happiest day of my life, because that was the day I screwed a friend of mine out of a bunch of money.

As I stood there looking at the beautiful water-fall, I wondered how many other people had stood there, and how many had candy corn "teeth" sticking out between their lips like I did.

I remember one night I was walking past Mom and Dad's room when I heard them talking about how they might not have enough money to pay their bills that month. I knew what I had to do. I went and got my piggy bank and buried it in the backyard, where they couldn't get their mitts on it.

The smell of Aunt Lucy's pies would make me come a-runnin'. But the sight of Aunt Lucy's face would make me run away.

When I was in the third grade, a bully at school started beating me up, every day. At first I didn't say anything, but then I told Dad. He got a real scared look on his face and asked if the bully had a big dad. I said I didn't know, but he still seemed scared, and just a few days later we moved to a new town.

Dad told me if anybody picked on me not to fight back, unless I knew the kid didn't have a dad or the dad was real small. Otherwise, he said, "just curl up in a ball."

I think the most beautiful sunset I ever saw was on page 4 and 5 of *The Book of Sunsets.*

O ne thing I always felt bad about was kicking Grandma in the head with my football shoes on. But what was her head doing right by the football like that? And how did the football get in her bed?

W hen I was a kid, the people next door had this little yappy poodle that I used to make fun of all the time. I thought it was real stupid-looking and annoying. But let me tell

you, I didn't make fun of it after the time it saved my life. How did it save my life? It's a long story. Too long to tell here. But I can tell you it was full of excitement and danger, and afterwards I never made fun of that poodle again.

Well, I suppose I can at least try to tell the story. I'm still not sure I believe it myself, so many strange and fantastic things happened. Briefly what happened, though, is this: I was walking across a vacant lot near my house when I heard a noise. I turned. You know what? This story is just too hard to try to tell here. Just believe it when I say that the poodle came out of nowhere to attack a cobra.

Where did the cobra come from? Okay, I guess I can at least tell that part. No, I'm going to change my mind again. It's just too hard to explain—although if I did explain it, you would be glued to the edge of your seat.

Maybe someday I'll tell the story of the poodle and the cobra. No, I won't. It's a good one though.

I knew Mrs. Stewart, our neighbor, was afraid of black cats, so one day I dressed up in a black cat costume and went over and mowed her lawn. Then I left. I think that cured her.

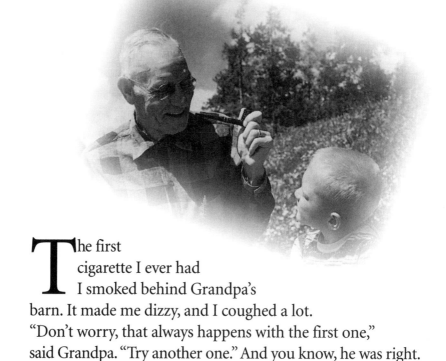

The first
cigarette I ever had
I smoked behind Grandpa's
barn. It made me dizzy, and I coughed a lot.
"Don't worry, that always happens with the first one,"
said Grandpa. "Try another one." And you know, he was right.

Every year at Christmastime a whole set of emotions sweeps over me—emotions which probably go back to my childhood.

The first emotion is wondering if I'm going to get any presents. Then it changes to "Hooray, I got some presents!" Then it changes to "Is that all the presents I got?"

I'll never forget the time the president came to our town. When I saw him go by, he looked so much older and sadder than I thought he was. Also, why was he driving an ice cream truck?

When I went for my first job interview, I guess I was pretty confident, because I told the guy who was interviewing me he was fired. I didn't get the job, but that isn't what bothered me. What bothered me was I found out a few months later that that guy was still working there. Hey, man, I fired you!

I think the things you remember most are the little things, like that little space guy I kept tied up down in the basement. That little guy was only about five inches tall! He used to beg me to untie his rope, but I knew he'd just run away if I did. I think the cat finally got him. But the cat had little burn marks on him, from where the space guy shot him with his little gun, before his ammo ran out.

I remember things like that.

I'll never forget the time we were at the beach and we buried Uncle Joe in the sand. Boy, did we get in trouble! In fact, we got arrested. It turns out you can't bury people at the beach. Only at the cemetery.

I couldn't believe it! Someone had stolen my new sled! My brand-new, all-white sled, with the runners I had painted white and the white tow-rope and my name written on the top, in white. I asked all of my so-called friends which one of them took it, but they all denied it. Finally, in the spring, right after the snow melted, the thief brought it back to where I had left it.

LEMONADE

5¢ .2¢

When I was about ten years old, we set up a lemonade stand on the sidewalk in front of our house. But we didn't sell many glasses, and after a few hours, we took it down. I think that was the first time I realized that the world doesn't give a damn about you or anything you do.

One year Dad decided he was going to take us on a "surprise vacation." We wouldn't know where we were going until we got there. We were all real excited when we piled into the station wagon early one morning. We went about five blocks, then we got in an accident at a four-way stop.

I guess it was a pretty good surprise, but why did we need all that camping gear?

I'll never forget my first true love. She was the most beautiful thing I had ever seen. From her dark, raven hair to her slender, yellow, scaly feet, she was all woman. She loved corn, and could eat it all day with her hard, yellowish lips. "Caw!" she would yell, as a joke, then flap her arms with delight.

One day, she was sitting on a fence, and some guy shot her.

There's always been a good explanation for everything. When that owl attacked Grandma and started biting her head, at first it didn't make any sense. Why would an owl attack Grandma? But then we found out later: a mouse was living in her hairdo.

I remember when we were kids, one of our favorite games was to play "pirate." We'd dress up like pirates. Then we'd go find an adult walking down the street and we'd go up to him and pull out our butcher knives, which we called "swords," and say, "We're pirates! Give us your money!" A lot of adults would pretend to be scared and give us their money. Others would suddenly run away, yelling for help. We played pirate until we were twenty or so.

If I could go back and change one thing in my life, I think it would be that time I found that one-dollar bill on the sidewalk. I would change it to a million-dollar bill.

When I gave the bellboy his tip, he just sort of snarled at me. So I gave him some more money, but he just kept snarling. More money, more snarling. Finally I realized, Hey, you're not the bellboy, this is a robbery!

I asked him anyway if he would carry my bag, but he wouldn't.

One day Dad asked me to go fishing with him. I got scared. I had the feeling he was going to try to drown me. I don't know why I thought that, because so far he had never tried to kill me. But he had never taken me fishing either, so I was suspicious.

When we got to the lake, he walked right up to it. "Hey, son, come here," he said. "Look at these minnows."

"Nice try, Dad—if that's your real name!" I yelled. Then I ran back to the car and locked myself in.

Dad never took me fishing again. So I think that proves my case.

M
om used to warn me that I could lose an eye playing with BB guns. But she never warned me that I could also lose my BB gun, which I did.

What started out to be a nice pleasant drive in the country turned into the "Afternoon from Hell."

First of all, when Marta and I were leaving, the cats looked at us like, "Where are you going?"

Then, when we were driving, we had to stop and get gas. So right there that's time taken away from looking at the scenery.

Then, when we get home, guess what the cats are doing? *Sleeping!*

Man, what next?

We asked Dad if we could have a trampoline, but he said no, that they were too dangerous and too expensive. But then we went and talked to the trampoline salesman at the store, and he said they weren't too expensive or dangerous. I think I'm still sorta mad at Dad for lying to us like that.

R emember when the teacher would forget to give the class homework and you'd raise your hand and tell her she forgot, there would always be people who would moan and complain. Didn't you hate those people?

Sunday was always Pancake Day in our family, because that was the day we'd all drive up to Pancake Mountain, and then maybe on the way home stop and get some pizza.

We'd always sing the same song, too, on the way home. It went like this:

There's nothing flatter
Than a pizza
Nothing you can make.
The only thing that might
Be flatter
Is a fish they call the hake!

I'll never forget the time my friend Stew went skydiving. Boy, what a mistake that was! First of all, his parachute didn't open. Second, we didn't have the right address, so before we got there we got lost and went driving all around for almost an hour. And third, when we finally did get there, Stew tried to back out and we had to talk him into going.

I don't think I received enough love when I was a child. And not just from my parents. From my other relatives, and my friends, and from strangers and from all the creatures of the world, including bugs.

I'll never forget the time I got caught stealing watermelons from old Mr. Barnslow's watermelon patch. I was with my friend Bobby. We were giggling so hard I thought I'd wet my pants!

At first we tried to steal two watermelons each, but they were too heavy and we dropped them, and that made us laugh even harder.

Finally, we each picked out a good one, and we were just about to sneak back through the fence when we heard a low, deep voice behind us. "Just where do you two think you're going with those watermelons?" I gulped and turned around. It was old Mr. Barnslow, pointing his shotgun at us.

Bobby dropped his watermelon, then pulled out the .38 revolver he kept in his waist, turned, and fired. But the turning must have thrown off his aim, because the shot only hit Mr. Barnslow in the thigh. Mr. Barnslow immediately fired both barrels at Bobby. One blast of buckshot missed entirely, but the other tore into Bobby's shoulder. He tried to fire back, but his shoulder was so torn up he couldn't raise his arm. Just as he was trying to switch to his left hand, Mr. Barnslow ran up and cracked him across the face with the butt of his shotgun. Bobby fell to the ground in a heap. Mr. Barnslow raised the butt of his gun to finish him off, but just then Bobby pulled out his hunting knife and plunged it into the farmer's big white belly.

After that, I don't think I stole watermelons for at least a year.

One Thanksgiving my parents did something I don't know if I can ever forgive them for. We were eating our turkey dinner when suddenly I realized I hadn't seen my pet turkey all day. "Where's Mister Gobble?" I asked.

Dad seemed confused. "Mister Gobble?"

"Yes," I said. "My turkey. The one I picked

out at the supermarket, and then after he thawed out I made him do a funny little turkey dance. Mister Gobble."

Dad's silence said it all. We were *eating* Mister Gobble! I ran crying from the table and locked myself in my room.

Later, Dad knocked on the door and said he had some dessert for me. When I opened the door, I couldn't believe it. It was a slice of Pumpkie, my pet pie!

2/16/11

I only played hooky one time, so I'll never forget it. I hid in the bushes right outside my classroom. And since the window was open, I could hear the teacher, so I went ahead and took notes. When the teacher asked a question, I raised my hand, but she couldn't see me.

I used to think Mom's biscuits were special, because she said she put a secret ingredient in them. Years later I asked her what the secret ingredient was, and she said it was "love." Right then I felt like the biggest sucker in the world.

When I looked up at the scoreboard, there were fifteen seconds left. It seemed like plenty of time, but it wasn't. Before I could get to the rest room, I had wet my pants.

I'll never forget the time Grandma tripped at the top of the stairs and fell all the way down and then rolled and hit her head against the front door. We all laughed and laughed, until we realized, Hey, she's not joking!

The first time I ever saw the ocean, I was real disappointed. "That's the ocean?!" I said. No, said Mom and Dad, that's just the parking lot. When we pulled into the lot, I was real disappointed in it.

It was hard to find a spot, and the spaces seemed way too narrow, in my book.

The ocean was okay, I guess, but I still can't get over how disappointing that parking lot was.

Every summer we'd get our baskets and buckets and go out into the hills and woods, looking for wild strawberries, blueberries, and blackberries. We never found any, though.

Kids don't need expensive new toys to have fun. A lot of times we would have just as much fun getting in my dad's car and letting off the emergency brake and just seeing where the car would go before it stopped.

I remember the first time I ever saw a shooting star I said, "What the hell is that?" But nowadays when I see one I just say, "What is that?" I leave off the "hell" part. Maybe when I'm old I'll just say, "Whazzit?"

The first time I ever tried to milk a cow at Grandpa's farm, I didn't even know which end of the cow to milk! Then I guess I got even dumber, because the next time I couldn't even find the barn. Then the last time, I just went out in the woods and lived, with no clothes.

A unt Lucy always used to win first prize at the county fair for her apple pie. It wasn't a real county fair—that's just what they called it at the mental home where she lived. And it wasn't a real apple pie either. Usually it was a ball of dough with tongue depressors and pieces of gum sticking out of it. Still, she won.

Maybe it's my imagination, but food seemed to taste better when I was a kid. Also, food would sing and dance and play musical instruments. But that could also have been my imagination.

My parents used to abandon me a lot as a child. In the morning, they'd take me to my school and then abandon me there, until school got out. Then at night, after they tucked me in bed, they'd abandon me and go to sleep in their own bedroom. Sometimes they'd let me sleep with them in their room, but if I started playing my guitar they'd take me back to my bedroom and abandon me again.

Once, they abandoned me for a whole week, at my grandparents' house.

I don't remember much at all from when I was born, except for the bright lights and being held upside down and being slapped hard on my bottom. Also, I remember thinking the doctor had a funny mustache, and when I grew up I would never have a mustache like that.

If you ever decide to go panning for gold, like my friend Bob and I did one time, here are a few tips: First of all, when you're leaving to go pan, don't lock your keys in your car. Then, when you go back in your house to get a coat hanger to open it, don't realize you also locked yourself out of your house.

Next, while you're standing there trying to figure out what to do, don't get attacked by a big swarm of biting flies. But if you do, don't go running to the house next door and pound on the door and the window, screaming for the neighbors to let you in, because it scares them and they just start screaming back and yelling for you to go away.

Finally, don't have a friend who has a nervous breakdown like Bob, because when the ambulance comes and you try to drive away in it so you can finally go panning, they get real mad at you.

When Dad found out the house was full of termites, he got real mad. But I was glad, because now I wouldn't have to go all the way to the woods to get termites for my termite farm.

In all the time I was growing up, I only saw Dad cry two times. After the first time, I didn't say anything. But after the second time I left a note on his dresser that said "See a psychiatrist." I don't know if he ever did, but at least I didn't see him cry again.

I remember the time I asked Grandpa what he did in the war. At first he didn't say anything. Then he pulled a frozen T-bone steak from under his shirt. "I stole this," he said.

"No," I said, "not the store, the *war*."

He showed me a red mark on his stomach and said he was wounded, but I think it was from the T-bone.

One year Dad decided he was going to save money on haircuts, so he bought an electric haircutter kit. At first everything went fine, but then he gave us haircuts. They were horrible. Then everything seemed to be going fine for a while, but then he gave us haircuts again. So I guess, mostly, it was a good idea.

3/25/10

When I was a kid, I used to think you could jump off the roof of our house using an umbrella as a parachute. I thought my little brother could, anyway.

Life is funny. One minute you're a little kid, running through a meadow, and the next, you're a skeleton, walking through a meadow, with dogs chasing you.

When my cousin Billy came and stayed at our house for a week, at first everything seemed okay. But then I started noticing things were missing. The first thing was a bag of garbage we kept under the kitchen sink. Then the piles of ashes and butts in the ashtrays. Then all the weeds in the yard.

I never said anything to him, but we never invited him back.

It was really sad when I went to visit my friend Jim at the state mental institution. He was convinced he was on a tropical island with no cares and no worries. It took me a long time to convince him that no, he was in a room with bare walls and a bare bed and he was wearing a straitjacket.

When
we were kids,
I used to make fun of
my friend Kevin whenever he had to go to
his piano lesson. But look where he is now and look
where I am. Actually, I don't know where he is now.
But look where I am, that's my point.

When I found the wallet in the road, I started wondering about the guy who owned it. Who was he? Was it William Gregory of 2407 Eastwood Lane, like the driver's license said, or was it someone else? And what was he going to spend the $220 on?

About a week later, I started wondering again about the wallet guy. What was he like? And where was he going to spend his five dollars?

The way I see it, kids need exercise more than they need ice cream. So when I worked as an ice cream man, driving an ice cream truck, I would try to drive fast enough that the kid couldn't catch me, but not so fast that he'd give up right away. Some kids will chase you for eight or nine blocks.

I think the biggest mistake I ever made in my life was not eating *all* of that guy's pie instead of just half of it, because he was in the rest room for at least another two or three minutes.

There used to be this bully who would demand my lunch money every day. Since I was smaller, I would give it to him. But then I decided to fight back. I started taking karate lessons. But then the karate lesson guy said I had to start paying him five dollars a lesson. So I just went back to paying the bully. Before I paid him, though, I would go into my karate stance, because that's all I learned before I got kicked out.

One time I was going to throw a surprise party for Marta, but the surprise ended up being on *me*. That's because the party seemed like too much trouble and I eventually gave up, and I was surprised to find out I was that lazy.

One afternoon, when I was about ten, I decided to walk over to the "wrong side of the tracks." At first I was a little scared. But then I noticed that the yards were nice, and so were the houses. In fact, most of the houses were better than those on our side of the tracks. A *lot* better.

W hen I told Dad I wanted a kite he said, "Okay, but instead of *buying* a kite, let's *make* one." So we did. Then, about a month later, we also made me a bicycle, but it blew away.

When I was about in the third grade I used to play with matches all the time. Then one day, something made me stop. I accidentally scraped one across a rough surface and it caught on fire!

"Hey, sport, how would you like to go for a drive in the country—just you and me?" Grandpa had hardly finished the question before I was in the front seat of that big Buick of his. It was a beautiful sunny day, perfect for cruising the back roads.

Suddenly we swerved off onto a narrow dirt road and skidded to a stop. Grandpa hustled me down into a gully, where this weird European-looking couple was waiting. They looked me up and down, even checking my teeth. Finally they told Grandpa, "No. No goot."

Grandpa said, "Yes, goot," but that didn't seem to satisfy them. Then Grandpa said okay, but they couldn't have the money back they had already paid him.

Then we got back in the car and drove home.

At summer camp one night it was my turn to tell a ghost story around the campfire. I started to tell this story about a murderer who has a hook for a hand, but then I saw that one of the kids sitting there had a hook instead of a hand. When I saw that, I let out a big scream and went running for my tent, as fast as my little legs could take me.

One weird thing that happened to me was one time I was in a plane that was landing and I suddenly stood up and yelled, "The plane's going to crash! The plane's going to crash!" The stewardess told me to sit down and be quiet, so I did.

The plane landed okay, but as we were all going to get our bags, I started yelling, "Our bags aren't going to be there! They're not gonna be there!" But they were, even Strappy.

So I rented one of those metal carts to put your bags on, and guess what happened? I crashed into another guy's cart.

So that's pretty weird, isn't it?

I remember the first time I ever went to the museum and saw the mummy. At first I was afraid of it. So, to get over my fear, I started pointing at the mummy and doing a funny little dance. But then I couldn't stop doing the dance. Something made me dance faster and faster until finally I fell on the floor. Even then I couldn't stop doing the dance. I flailed about helplessly, yelling some weird Egyptian words! Then I think I passed out, from hitting my head on the marble floor.

Now, I'm happy to say, I'm no longer afraid of the mummy, mainly because I don't go there anymore.

Sometimes it's hard to tell if something is actually a memory, or you just dreamed it. So I asked my boss if I called him a lying, stinking thief, or I just dreamed it, and he said I just dreamed it. Whew, that was close.

I guess we were kinda poor when we were kids, but we didn't know it. That's because my dad always refused to let us look at the family's financial records.

I'm not so sure it's good to think back to my childhood memories, because I end up feeling happy and sad at the same time, and that gives me a weird "neutral" feeling.